Original title:
Melon Days

Copyright © 2025 Creative Arts Management OÜ
All rights reserved.

Author: Lucas Harrington
ISBN HARDBACK: 978-1-80586-352-6
ISBN PAPERBACK: 978-1-80586-824-8

## Fluid Sunlight

The sun spills laughter on the ground,
Shiny and golden, it dances around.
Children giggle, a carefree spree,
As sticky fingers climb a tall tree.

A slick little slide made of bright rays,
Bouncing like balls in jubilant plays.
Yellow and green, a playful blend,
Chasing our shadows, we never descend.

## Harvest Moonlight and Juicy Delights

Under the moon, we gather and cheer,
With bowls overflowing, we hold them near.
Splashes of sweetness drip down our chins,
Laughter erupts as the spillage begins.

The night air's thick with fruity delight,
A feast of flavors, a spectacular sight.
In the glow of the moon, we make a toast,
To the candy from earth, we love the most.

## The Dance of Summer's Bounty

A party of colors on the green grass,
Wiggles and jigs as the time will pass.
With every bite, giggles burst free,
Our taste buds are twirling in joyful glee.

We shuffle and sway, making grand messes,
In a world full of juice, we learn our lessons.
Taste and dance, that's the summer tune,
Under a warm and gleeful afternoon.

### **Savoring the Season's Embrace**

Time for a treasure hunt all about,
Giggles echo as friends jump about.
Sticky hands reach for blissful bites,
With whispers of joy on warm summer nights.

Baskets in tow, we race with delight,
Finding sweet wonders that sparkle so bright.
In every scoop, a story unfolds,
As we treasure the warmth that summer holds.

## Memory's Palette

In the garden, colors splash,
Green and pink in a dandy clash.
The taste of sweetness fills the air,
While bees buzz by without a care.

A splash of juice, a silly grin,
Sticky fingers, where to begin?
Laughter echoes, a juicy splat,
Who knew fruit could make us that?

## A Taste of Tranquility

Under the sun, we sit and munch,
Squirrels nearby plotting their lunch.
With each bite, a giggle escapes,
As juice rolls down like silly drapes.

Friends toss seeds like tiny darts,
Hitting shadows, stealing hearts.
Nature smiles in shades of glee,
Sweetness wraps us like a spree.

## Summer's Colorful Feast

Bright and bold, the colors shine,
In every slice, a taste divine.
Seeds like treasure in the mix,
Throw them far, make silly tricks.

Our picnic spread, a rainbow flair,
Ants march in, we do not care.
Laughter rings out, a joyful beat,
Life's simple joys are hard to beat.

## **As the Sun Melts**

Daylight dances, shadows sway,
Fruit fun rolls in, come what may.
With every bite, a joke is birthed,
This happiness, our own true worth.

The sunset blushes, colors bloom,
Sweetness lingers while squirrels zoom.
Everyone smiles, no room for frowns,
In this moment, joy abounds.

## **Slices of Euphoria**

In the sun, we twirl and spin,
With juicy joy that draws us in.
Splashes of nectar on our face,
A sticky, sweet, delightful race.

Chasing seeds that fly away,
Laughter bursts, we yell 'hooray!'
Splatters land on noses round,
In this bliss, pure fun is found.

## **The Color of Laughter**

Sipping smiles under the shade,
Bright hues dance, never fade.
A patchwork quilt of juicy bites,
Where every giggle ignites delights.

Funny faces with juice on chins,
The laughter builds, nobody wins.
While sticky fingers wave in glee,
In this sweetness, we're all carefree.

## Hidden Treasures of the Field

In the garden, secrets lie,
As we peek and giggle, oh my!
Beneath the leaves, a prize awaits,
A round delight that tempts the fates.

Tugging gently, it rolls away,
Playing hide-and-seek all day.
We tumble over foot and tail,
In this treasure hunt, we prevail.

## Nature's Golden Hour

As the sun dips low to play,
We gather for the fray today.
Golden globes with laughter flare,
Under twinkling stars, unaware.

With giggles carried on the breeze,
We dance around, feel at ease.
Beneath the dusk, our joy expands,
Savoring summer's happy bands.

## The Taste of Sunbeams

In fields of gold, we laugh and play,
A fruity feast on a summer's day.
With each sweet bite, the giggles rise,
Sunlit joy, beneath bright skies.

The juice just drips, what a delight,
Sticky fingers, oh what a sight!
A burst of laughter, sticky and grand,
Sharing slices hand in hand.

## Refreshing Breezes

A gentle breeze whispers through the trees,
Tickling noses with a pleasant tease.
We dance and twirl, feeling so spry,
Chasing the shadows that flit nearby.

With every breeze, a cheer erupts,
Laughter floats as the fun corrupts.
Who knew that air could taste so sweet,
When shared with friends, it's quite the treat!

## Sweetness in Abundance

A basket full of laughter, spilling with cheer,
Each slice brings smiles, each bite draws near.
Juicy treasures, oh what a score,
Savor the sweetness, we all want more!

Fingers sticky, we grin and sigh,
As fruit-filled giggles float to the sky.
Biting into bliss, we cannot wait,
To spread the joy on each plate!

## A Symphony of Flavors

In a patch of sweetness, we gather 'round,
With fruity notes that astound.
Each drip and drool, a melody more,
A joyful chorus we can't ignore.

The colors burst, a painter's dream,
Slicing and sharing, bursting at the seam.
With laughter ringing, we sing along,
A fruity fiesta, where we all belong!

## Beneath the Green Canopy

Under leaves that shimmer bright,
We dodge the fruits that take flight.
Laughter echoes through the trees,
As sticky juice attracts the bees.

A splat! A squish! A fruity fight,
Squeals abound, oh what a sight!
The ground is stained with hues so bold,
A sweet mishap, or so I'm told.

## **Tantalizing Summer Evenings**

At dusk we gather, all aglow,
With sticky fingers, giggles flow.
An army of seeds we toss and cheer,
Each one a tiny laugh, I fear.

The sun dips down, and we all sway,
To the tune of fun on a sunny day.
In juicy puddles, we take a leap,
Summer sweetness, oh, it runs deep.

**Embracing the Essence of Warmth**

Chasing shadows, the sun beats down,
With laughter loud, we scoot around.
Tumbles happen, with a squeak and yell,
A slip on juice, a fruity farewell!

The air is thick with cheer and zest,
In this wild orchard, we feel blessed.
Giggles burst like softening fruit,
In this sweet chaos, we find our root.

## Whispered Secrets of the Orchard

Whispers dance on warm summer air,
Secret patches, we venture to share.
Rolling in laughter, we tumble about,
A fruity surprise, and we squeal with doubt.

Underneath the trees, we plot and scheme,
With juice-dripped chins, indulging our dream.
In sunny hideaways, we find our play,
Life is a fruit salad, come join the ballet!

## A Slice of Sunshine

In the market, fruits on parade,
A big round one, my plans are laid.
I'll wear a hat, I'll grab a slice,
Spilling juice, oh, that's so nice!

Spots of yellow, a burst of green,
Eating fruit like a juicy queen.
Laughing loud with friends at play,
Sipping sunshine, all day, hooray!

## Green Dreams and Golden Gleams

In a patch, all squishy sweet,
Found a treasure, what a treat!
Rolling 'round in sunny cheer,
With my friends, I hold it dear.

Glorious globes, a race we run,
Twirling 'round, oh, what fun!
A splash of juice, a drippy grin,
In this world, the best to win!

## Dewdrops on Rind

Morning dew on vibrant skin,
Nature's giggle, let's begin.
Grab a slice, it's time to share,
Each bite bursting, joy laid bare.

Tomfoolery with seeds galore,
Launching them, we shout for more!
Scattered laughs, a fruity fight,
Ending the day in pure delight.

## The Lullaby of Summer Fruits

Underneath the sky so blue,
Joking 'round as we all chew.
Silly faces, sticky hands,
Swaying lightly, summer plans.

Quiet whispers, secret dreams,
In the shade, the laughter beams.
Summer whispering soft and sweet,
With juicy treats, life is a feat!

## **Crystal Drops of Sunshine**

Under the beam of golden light,
The puddles laugh, a silly sight.
A splash of joy, a playful dance,
We chase the rain, not caring for chance.

In fields where giggles soar so free,
Like jumping beans, we leap with glee.
With berries ripe, we feast and play,
In a world where we tumble each day.

## Patchwork of Pleasures

Laughter blooms like flowers bright,
In a quilt of fun, stitched tight.
Chocolate stains on everyone's face,
Sweet sticky fingers in this race.

Picnic ants parade on the ground,
While merry songs of birds resound.
A sprightly breeze whispers so low,
Catching the moments as we throw.

## The Chill of Sweetness

A frosty treat on a summer's day,
With spoons like swords, we laugh and play.
The coolness drips, we race the tide,
Sticky giggles, what a fun ride!

With bellyaches and joy we share,
Cones melt fast, but we don't care.
Each bite a burst, a silly cheer,
We lick the sweet, and dance without fear.

## Memory's Orchard

In an orchard filled with vibrant hues,
We toss our worries like old shoes.
Fruits may tumble, but so do we,
Rolling through laughter, wild and free.

Under the branches, we make a spree,
Whispers of joy, as sweet as can be.
With every bite, a story we tell,
In this orchard of joy, all is well.

## Juicy Whispers of Summer

In a field of green, we roam,
Chasing giggles, far from home.
Wobbly fruit in the sun so bright,
Squeezing laughter, pure delight.

Seeds like confetti, fly through the air,
Sticky fingers, no time to care.
With every bite, a burst of cheer,
Making memories that linger near.

A splash of juice, a funny face,
Rolling around, a playful chase.
Sunshine laughter fills the day,
In fruity games, we love to play.

Time drips slowly, sweet and round,
As joy spills forth from the ground.
In the warmth, our worries fade,
As we dance in the sunshine parade.

## The Sweetness Beneath the Skin

Underneath the sun's warm glow,
A treasure waits, so ripe, we know.
Belly laughs with every bite,
Juicy giggles, pure delight.

With every slice, a splash we make,
Frolicking joy, wide smiles awake.
A fruit-filled feast, our favorite game,
Squirting sweetness, calling names.

Caught in laughter, we can't resist,
A comedy of juice and twist.
The seeds shoot out, like tiny jets,
In summer bliss, no regrets yet.

Shady spots where shadows play,
In the cool, we laugh away.
Beneath the skin, so soft and bright,
Summer's sweetness brings delight.

## **Sun-Kissed Reflections**

Beneath the sun, we lounge and grin,
Juicy shades of fun begin.
A picnic spread, a splash of cheer,
With each round bite, we steer clear.

Reflections dance upon our face,
Fruit-filled smiles, a playful chase.
Laughter bubbles, shades of gold,
Stories of summer waiting to be told.

Bright colors burst, a visual treat,
Happy hearts skip with the beat.
In the warmth, we find our song,
Playing around where we belong.

As evening falls, fun never ends,
In juicy moments, sunshine sends.
Together in joy, we take a stand,
Creating memories, hand in hand.

## Harvesting Laughter on Hot Afternoons

Hot afternoons, the sun's a clown,
In juicy patches, we jump around.
With every taste, we laugh and sigh,
As sticky goodness drips nearby.

Hats on heads, our shields of fun,
Chasing shadows, we're on the run.
Fruit juice rivers, laughter flows,
In the heat, our playful woes.

We squeeze the bits, make funny faces,
In this harvest, joy embraces.
Witty puns and silly cheers,
Echoing softly through the years.

As the sun dips low, we stay afloat,
On joy's big wave, we love to gloat.
In every slice, we find delight,
Harvesting laughter into the night.

## Sun-Kissed Harvest

Under the sun so bright,
Laughter fills the air,
Fruits roll in a playful fight,
Sticky hands everywhere.

Juicy bites, oh what a thrill,
Seeds fly in gleeful arcs,
Chasing friends down the hill,
Squeals echo with the larks.

Giggles burst from every side,
Water bottles spill and splash,
Hidden treasures may abide,
Who knew juice could cause such a crash?

As shadows lengthen in the park,
The bounty's piling high,
With every funny remark,
Who could say goodbye?

## **The Scent of Ripe Dreams**

In fields where laughter grows,
Sweet perfumes drift along,
Ripe fruit, as funny as it goes,
Bees dance to a silly song.

The juice drips down their cheeks,
Smiles brighter than the sun,
Despite the mess, oh how it peaks,
Who knew fun could weigh a ton?

Rolling tumblers filled with cheer,
Chasing flavors on the breeze,
Like summer, bright and clear,
Nothing here is meant to tease.

With every scent, a funny tale,
Of slips and slides on grass,
Joyfulness fills up the vale,
In these moments, time won't pass.

## Nectar on the Breeze

Catch the waves of laughter's tune,
As fruits tumble down the lane,
Bright colors those silly balloons,
Hovering like they feel no pain.

A sip too sweet, they chase it fast,
Cups overflow with joy so pure,
Moments fleeting but meant to last,
In this giggle-filled grandeur.

Kids and pets all run about,
In a game of frisbee fruit,
Laughter's melody, no doubt,
Who knew juice made such a hoot?

With sticky fingers, the day won't end,
More fun waits as they play,
Life is sweet when we all blend,
Into the nectar of the day.

## Orchard's Lullaby

As evening falls, the sun dips low,
Whimsical tales float in the air,
The orchard whispers, soft and slow,
With giggles, they shake their hair.

Tanning grass and chuckles thrive,
As shadows stretch their limbs,
Each chuckle feels so alive,
Echoing like familiar hymns.

Gather round for mem'ries bright,
Juicy bites fill hearts with glee,
In this orchard's fading light,
Funny stories roam so free.

When the stars begin to twinkle,
All the laughter starts to fade,
But in dreams, those jests will sprinkle,
Sweet remnants of the fun we've made.

## Radiance in Every Bite

In sunlit patches, they glow bright,
A fruit so juicy, pure delight.
With every crunch, we laugh and play,
While sticky fingers slip away.

The juice drips down, a cheeky smile,
We race to finish, oh, it's worthwhile!
The seeds fly out like tiny drops,
We giggle loud, who wants the tops?

Friends gather round, the fun ignites,
Caught in the sweetness, oh, what sights!
Each slice a treasure, vibrant and sweet,
In our fruit party, we can't be beat!

Oh, how we savor the flavors, so well,
In each little bite, we hear stories to tell.
Laughter erupts with every big bite,
Radiance shines, oh what a delight!

## The Ritual of Slices

Gather the crew, the time is here,
To chop and slice without any fear.
A dance of fruits, a wild embrace,
In the kitchen, there's laughter and grace.

With every slice, we share a giggle,
Watch out for juice—oh, what a wiggle!
Chopping boards hold our sticky fate,
Who knew fruit could generate such bait?

A sprinkle of salt, let's not be shy,
We play with flavors as time goes by.
In circles we sit, spoons in our hands,
The ritual's joy, the best of our plans!

We toss the scraps to the eager bin,
And savor the sweetness, that's where we win.
A toast to the slices, oh what a cheer,
In each crunchy moment, the laughter's sincere!

## **Fields of Flavor**

Out in the open, fields wave and sway,
Colors so vibrant, they steal the day.
We roam the rows, wild and free,
Searching for surprises for you and me.

With baskets in hand, we giggle and prance,
Who knew fruit could lead to such a dance?
A plump one here, a small one there,
Gathering joy, without a care.

The flavors mingle, a party so grand,
A bite of sweetness, it's all been planned.
Nature's own candy, handmade delight,
In fields of flavor, everything feels right!

Oh, how we cherish the fun that we keep,
Amongst lush greenery, not a hint of sleep.
In every harvest, a laughter-filled cheer,
Fields of delight, let's return each year!

## **A Serenade of Seeds**

Tiny black dots in a sea of sweet,
Unruly mess, but that's our treat.
We share our finds, with laughs and shouts,
In a chorus of flavors, fun never doubts.

Each seed a story, a tangled thread,
As we munch away, the laughter spread.
From bites of fruit, we thread the fun,
With every giggle, our hearts will run.

Unleashing joy, every seed's a clue,
Playful adventures, just me and you.
A serenade of crunches and cheers,
What a symphony after all these years!

So here's to the seeds, the joy they bring,
In laughter's reminder, let your heart sing.
For in each little fruit, and every dance,
We find our joy, we take a chance!

## Shades of Green and Orange

Under the sun, colors so bright,
Green and orange, what a sight!
Laughter bursts, just like juicy treats,
Summer giggles dance on our feet.

With every bite, the fun spills out,
Juicy drips, and friends will shout!
A sticky fight with fruit so fine,
Who knew tummies could be so divine?

Beneath the trees, we take our place,
Orange stains paint every face!
We wear our joy like a funny crown,
Tasting happiness all around.

Rolling in laughter, we share our cheer,
That zesty fruit has brought us here!
So raise a slice, let the giggles flow,
In this world of green and orange glow.

## **Nectar Dripping from Joy**

Sweet nectar flows, a sticky mess,
Laughter bursts, oh what a bless!
We gather close, in the sunny rays,
Sipping joy from summer's trays.

Chasing droplets, a race so fast,
Forget the chores, we're having a blast!
Splattered smiles and fruit-filled cheeks,
This joy of ours never peaks.

With friends around, the giggles soar,
Nectar drips, who could ask for more?
We toast to fun, on our silly spree,
Where laughter grows like a buzzing bee.

So come and join this fruity parade,
Life's too short for being afraid!
We'll sip and spill all day and night,
For nectar drips in pure delight.

## The Tapestry of Taste

A canvas bright, we take the chance,
To taste the sun, let's start the dance!
Layers of flavor, summery cheer,
Creating smiles from ear to ear.

Patchwork of colors, a joyful spread,
Taste the laughter, enough said!
Strawberry stripes and kiwi dreams,
Woven together, bursting at the seams.

Fruits on sticks, a wobbly sight,
Funny faces in pure delight!
In every slice, there's joy to trace,
A tasty journey, a funny embrace.

So let's raise a glass to this tasty show,
With every munch, let your laughter grow!
A tapestry of joy, woven tight,
In the flavors of delight and light.

## Basking in Sweetness

We lounge outside, full of cheer,
Basking in sweetness, summer's here!
Fruit dripping down, a comical mess,
Who knew sticky could taste its best?

Let's take a bite, and share a grin,
With juicy chunks, let the fun begin!
Watermelon wedges, all around,
Funny faces, laughter abound.

Happiness spills like juice from a cup,
Sipping the sunshine, we can't get enough!
Rolling on grass, the joy we find,
With fruity treasures, we're feeling blind.

So grab a friend and join this spree,
Life is sweet, just like our spree!
Basking in flavors that can't be beat,
In this world, without a seat.

## Garden of Colorful Wonders

In a plot where laughter grows,
Colors dance as mischief flows.
Bouncing fruits with silly grins,
Hide and seek beneath the skins.

Bees wear caps, all dressed to play,
Tickled petals, bold display.
Worms in suits tell jokes galore,
Nature's stage, forever more.

Cheeky peppers crack a joke,
While carrots giggle, roots provoke.
Sunflowers wink from high above,
Each bloom a symbol of true love.

Rabbits hop with giddy cheer,
Rolling in the mud, oh dear!
Cuckoo clouds drift overhead,
What a place to dance and tread!

**Sunkissed Dreams**

Golden rays bring silly schemes,
Fun and laughter, bursting beams.
Fruits round and jolly, swaying slow,
Chasing shadows, all aglow.

Bumblebees wear shades of cool,
Sipping nectar by the pool.
Lemonade stands with funny signs,
"Try our drinks, they're worth your dines!"

Flip-flops flapping in the breeze,
Sunburnt noses bring you keys.
Close your eyes, and take a leap,
Into dreams where giggles creep.

Every sunset wraps in gold,
Tales of folly, truths retold.
With each night, the laughter stays,
In our hearts, these sunny ways.

## A Splash of Vivid Green

In fields so bright, a lively scene,
Frogs in ties, a vibrant green.
Splashing puddles, dancing feet,
Cucumbers waltz, oh what a treat!

Clouds wear hats, so fluffy wide,
While sprightly leaves flip side to side.
Radishes laugh, their cheeks so red,
In this joyful green, go ahead!

Pickles roll and tease the sun,
While wandering thoughts make it all fun.
Whisked away on a breeze of cheer,
Adventure calls, the time is near!

Twirling vines in quirky spins,
Nature's laughter always wins.
A garden playhouse, wild and free,
Join the party, come with me!

## Twilight's Tantalizing Treats

Fireflies dance, a glittering show,
While strawberries blush, stealing the glow.
Moonlit laughs, a flavorful night,
Toothaches waiting, oh what a sight!

Cakes on tables, icing dreams,
While silly shadows plot their schemes.
Cookies tumble, fresh from the oven,
Whirl in giggles, hearts a-lovin'.

Laughter echoes, all around,
As playful spirits leap and bound.
In the garden where flavors twine,
Twilight whispers, "All is fine!"

Desserts so grand, they steal the show,
Under stars with a lovely glow.
In this world, where joy's the key,
Join the feast, it's paradise, you see!

# The Taste of Nostalgia

In a patch so wide and bright,
Laughter bounces in the light.
Juicy smiles in every slice,
Childhood memories, oh so nice.

Spilling seeds and sticky hands,
Sun-kissed skin and sandy strands.
Scoops of joy from nature's treat,
Every taste feels like a cheat.

Bellyaches from laughter tried,
Running round in summer's pride.
Every bite, a grand parade,
Underneath the sunset's shade.

As we feast on the delight,
Friendship blooms, a pure invite.
In the feast of summer's bliss,
Every moment, we won't miss.

## Sunlit Adventures

A picnic spread beneath the sun,
Silly games and jokes for fun.
Tasting fruits with laughter near,
Chasing dreams without a fear.

On a blanket, oh so wide,
Sharing secrets side by side.
Each sweet bite a breath of cheer,
Time to smile, no worries here.

Watch the clouds as they parade,
Sprinkled snacks in a grand charade.
Cucumber hats and berry crowns,
All our laughter knows no bounds.

In this world of sweet delight,
Every wrong feels oh so right.
We'll remember this, we swear,
Sunlit joy beyond compare.

## Daytime Decadence

Feasting like royalty in the sun,
Spoonfuls of laughter, oh what fun!
Melting treats that dance and sway,
Delicious chaos, on display.

Friends around, the stories flow,
Wiggly giggles, heads held low.
Slipping on juice, what a show,
Who knew snacks could steal the glow?

We twirl and spin in pure delight,
With every bite, our hearts take flight.
Catching drops like candy rain,
Here's to laughter—once again!

Though sun may set, the fun won't fade,
Memory's recipe, sweetly made.
Hold on tight, we're in this race,
To taste the joy, to find our place.

## Sweet Tangents

Beneath the sun, we twist and twirl,
Fruit-filled dreams begin to whirl.
Silly faces, silly games,
Every moment, joy reclaims.

Giggles burst like ripe, sweet fruit,
Sticky fingers, a playful loot.
Sun hats crooked on our heads,
Chasing shadows, laughter spreads.

Lemonade rivers flow, oh dear,
Splashing fun, we cheer and cheer.
Every twist and turn's a ride,
Together on this joyful glide.

With every bite, we just might find,
A world so bright and sweetly blind.
So let's savor every taste,
In this wonderland, no haste.

## Harvest Moon Serenade

The moon hums sweetly, quite out of tune,
Laughter spills under a harvest moon.
Giggling shadows play hide and seek,
Jokes about fruits, oh, what a week!

Silly hats on a bumpy ride,
Sipping juice, with friends by my side.
Jumping into a patch of cheer,
With every slip, comes a hearty cheer!

Scarecrows dance in cotton clothes,
Wobbling, laughing, everybody knows.
The stars join in this playful jest,
A night to remember, simply the best!

Around the bonfire, stories flow,
Of funny mishaps from long ago.
With every chuckle, the warmth grows strong,
As we celebrate, with friends, we belong.

**Sweet Recollections**

In a garden bright, where giggles bloom,
Remembering times when we faced our doom.
With sticky hands and laughter loud,
We danced in circles, oh so proud!

Chasing the sun with our silly schemes,
Running through fields, living our dreams.
Fingers in pies, a sugar surprise,
Making a mess to our great demise!

Cool breezes whisper past our ears,
Tales of fun from yesteryears.
Oh, the flavors, the joy, the laughter,
We'd trade those moments for nothing after!

A snapshot paused, a moment's grace,
Every smile etched on each child's face.
Through clumsy moments and sweet delight,
We stitched our memories in the twilight.

## Fields of Delight

Among the greens, where we rolled and tumbled,
Laughter echoed, and our plans crumbled.
Backpacks heavy with treats galore,
Filling our hearts, we always wanted more!

Silly antics in the bright sunshine,
Creating chaos, all of us in line.
A splash of juice, a sticky face,
Running for cover, a frantic race!

Butterflies giggle as we chase them down,
Silly faces in a daisy crown.
With squeals of joy, we leap and bound,
In every corner, more fun is found!

Sunset paints the sky in hues,
As we sit down, sharing our views.
With every story, giggles ignite,
Fields of delight, our hearts take flight!

**Vintage Summer Memories**

Old photographs in a faded stack,
Remember the fun, there's no looking back.
With polka-dot dresses and goofy hats,
Lost in the moment, with cheerful spats!

Running barefoot on the gravel roads,
Our laughter echoing, lifting our loads.
Sticky fingers from summer treats,
Finding mischief in bustling streets!

Skipping stones by the shimmering lake,
Each plop a memory, more fun to make.
Drawing silly hearts in the sand,
With every wave, friendship's grand!

We'll raise a toast to those vintage days,
With a pinch of sugar and silly phrases.
Laughter lingers where love resides,
In summer's embrace, joy never hides!

## The Painter's Palette of Nature

In fields where colors mix and play,
Bright greens and yellows come out to sway.
Nature's brush just loves to tease,
A splatter here, a splash with ease.

Who knew the sun could drip like paint?
As critters giggle, no time to faint.
A canvas larger than all the shops,
With laughter rising, it never stops.

Each drop of dew a playful prank,
They bounce around, and never tank.
The clouds giggle, painting skies,
In this art, the joy just flies.

So let's skip through this vibrant spree,
With every hue, we find the key.
In nature's gallery, we take a bow,
To the silly colors that show us how!

## Soft Hues of Summer

The sun spills warm, like syrup on toast,
A sticky smile, we love it most.
Lemons laughing from the trees,
"A squeeze! A splash!"—a summer tease.

Children chase the vector of light,
While ants parade in a funny sight.
They march in line, so precise and true,
Racing for crumbs—just look at those two!

Picnics danced with laughter bright,
As sandwiches vanish out of sight.
The juice runs down, like giggles so sweet,
A playful summer, no need for a seat!

We toast our drinks, they clink and cheer,
"Here's to sunshine and laughter, my dear!"
In soft hues of joy, we find our groove,
With each hearty laugh, we keep the move!

## Chronicles of Abundance

In gardens brimming with cheerful sights,
Veggies plotting their silly heights.
Carrots chuckle, and tomatoes grin,
"I'm the juiciest!"—let the games begin!

Watermelons rolling like comets through space,
With every bounce, they pick up pace.
The squash perform like a grand ballet,
As zucchinis break into spontaneous play!

"Catch me if you can!" the peas declare,
As they hop along without a care.
Pumpkins wink from their lofty throne,
In the kingdom of green, they've surely grown.

So gather round for this harvest fest,
With laughter and bounty, we are blessed.
Each bite a story, each taste a shout,
In this funny world, we dance about!

## **Radiant Reflections**

In fields of green, we dance and sway,
With fruits so sweet, what a wild play!
Laughter erupts, like seeds in breeze,
Each slice brings joy, like sunshine's tease.

A picnic feast beneath the sun,
With juicy bites, oh, so much fun!
Sticky hands and silly grins,
The game of who can eat more wins!

The juice must flow, it's quite a sight,
As friends all gather, pure delight.
We juggle laughs, like fruit on plates,
A day of bliss, where humor waits.

When evening falls and shadows play,
We share our tales from this crazy day.
With seeds in teeth and hearts so light,
Our radiant smiles shine through the night.

## Sunshine Surprises

Splashing bright, the sun in cheer,
With fruity smiles far and near.
Unexpected laughs in every bite,
Oh, the joy of a summer's light!

A fruit fight breaks, with giggles loud,
Everyone joins in, feeling proud.
The sweetest chaos, what a spree,
In fruity happiness, wild and free!

Shadows stretch like silly strings,
As we pretend that we have wings.
Each chuckle's ripe, each moment gold,
These silly memories never get old.

When darkness falls, we'll reminisce,
About the laughter and fruity bliss.
A day of mischief, oh what a prize,
Packed with sunshine's sweet surprise!

## Meadow Melodies

In a meadow bright, tunes resound,
With every bite, joy is found.
Silly songs of the juicy joy,
Of youthful laughter, girl and boy.

The breeze carries giggles, oh so sweet,
As we waddle around on sticky feet.
A symphony of crunch and cheer,
No worries here, just fun and beer!

Dancing petals sway with grace,
But watch the fruit fly all over the place!
With splashes of color and laughter anew,
This meadow stage, a vibrant view.

With twilight's glow, our voices sing,
About the day's amusing fling.
Happiness echoes, pure as day,
These melodies lead our hearts astray.

## Fragrant Days

With scents of summer in our air,
Each colorful fruit brings laughter's dare.
We toss and catch, and what a sight,
The aroma's charm brings pure delight!

A smorgasbord of flavors burst,
In fruity fun, we quench our thirst.
The sun-drenched laughter fills the space,
Each chuckle shared, a happy race.

Hiccups from laughter make us pause,
As we debate which fruit's the cause.
With each bright flavor, we explore,
Group giggles echo, and we want more!

With fading light, our stories blend,
Of fragrant days, where fun won't end.
The memories linger like a sweet glaze,
In our hearts forever, those fragrant days.

## A Chorus of Refreshing Bliss

In sunlit fields where laughter grows,
The fruit parade, a silly show.
With every bite, a wiggly grin,
Juicy joy made out of skin.

The picnic spreads of squishy fun,
Water fights, we laugh and run.
Each splash a burst of cheery cheer,
Refreshment's song is all we hear.

So grab your slice, don't hesitate,
For sticky hands, it's never late.
In every seed, a joke we find,
A taste of sunshine, sweet and kind.

With every crunch, our giggles blend,
To every slice, we're good old friends.
So lift your forks and cheer away,
To this bright fruit-filled holiday!

## Crooked Pathways and Fruits

On twisted paths, the crows do caw,
We trip on roots, it's quite the draw.
A bounce, a tumble, a berry stain,
We laugh it off, despite the pain.

With wagging tails, the dogs parade,
Through patches where the colors fade.
Bananas slip and oranges roll,
Each fruit a prank to lift the soul.

We chase the squirrels who steal our snack,
They scamper fast, no looking back.
Each burst of color, nature's glee,
Provides a chuckle, wild and free.

So wander now, embrace the sill,
In crooked paths, we find the thrill.
With every step, let laughter swirl,
In every fruit, a fruity twirl!

## Daydreams of the Orchard

Beneath the branches, shadows dance,
As bees and blooms all take a chance.
In laughter, daydreams take their flight,
Surreal moments, pure delight.

A cider spill, a bobbing head,
A playful game, but toes are sped.
With plump and round, they bounce around,
As chuckles echo, joy is found.

We float away on fruity whims,
Painted skies and happy grins.
And in each sip of nature's brew,
The sweetness swells, refreshment too.

So gather here, and join the fun,
In orchard dreams, we're never done.
The worlds we make, so wild and free,
Are bursting forth with silliness, you see!

## The Aura of Juicy Simplicity

In a bowl of colors, joy resides,
Where laughter lurks and fun abides.
With peels and seeds, we dive right in,
A messy feast—a cheeky grin.

The juice that dribbles down our chin,
A tart surprise, twirls fun within.
With wiggly spoons, we scoop and share,
The simple pleasure fills the air.

Old stories blend with fruity laughs,
As summertime breaks into sweet halves.
In sunlit patches where we play,
The day's simplicity steals the sway.

So gather close, let spirits soar,
In every bite, we crave for more.
The essence sweet, in memory laid,
In joyful bumbles, time won't fade!

## Days Bathed in Nectar

In the garden, we all roam,
Smiling as we dread the foam.
Sticky fingers, hands so bright,
Sipping sweetness, pure delight.

Splashes here and splashes there,
Laughter floats upon the air.
Wobbling on our little toes,
Chasing juice from modest rows.

Sunburnt cheeks and giggles loud,
In the chaos, feeling proud.
Sweetness tricks us, oh so sly,
As laughter floats to dizzy high.

Sticky naps when day is done,
Mirth and juice, we had such fun!

## **Echoes of the Orchard**

Beneath the tree, we plot and scheme,
Dreaming of that big sweet dream.
Pits and seeds in every grin,
Who will dare to take a spin?

Giggles echo, whispers fly,
Orchard tales beneath the sky.
Ripe surprise in every bite,
Who knew that green could taste so bright?

Friends are thieves, oh what a game,
Sneaking bites, it's all the same.
Juicy dribbles down the chin,
With each grin, we can't help win!

As the sun begins to fade,
We'll share secrets that we've made.

## Summer's Sweet Serenade

A tune of joy, the season sings,
With every bite, the pleasure clings.
Purveyors of the summer's feast,
A symphony to say the least.

Sipping nectar, oh so sly,
Imagining the clouds go by.
Bouncing bells, a cheerful sound,
In every slice, pure joy is found.

Chasing shadows, laughter bold,
Juicy secrets, tales retold.
Flavors dancing, nothing bland,
Caught up in a sticky band.

As daylight bows to starlit grace,
Sweet aromas still embrace.

## Juicy Whispers of August

August brings its merry cheer,
In the sun, we reappear.
Floating dreams of fruity fun,
With every laugh, we brightly run.

Crisp delights as cousins tease,
Slurping loudly, if you please.
Seeds like landmines in our chase,
Avoiding them is quite a race.

Bouncing treats from hand to hand,
Mishaps turned to joy so grand.
With summer's glow upon our face,
In the nectar, we find our place.

As evening falls, we shout hooray,
This cheerful life is here to stay!

## **A Canvas of Sun-kissed Bliss**

In gardens bright, with laughter's cheer,
The fruits we pick, so sweet and clear.
With sticky hands and grins so wide,
We feast and play, our joy can't hide.

A splash of juice, it drips and swirls,
As summer spins, our hair in curls.
We toss and catch, the juicy treat,
A playful game, oh, what a feat!

Sunshine dances on our toes,
With every bite, the laughter flows.
A seed-spitting show, we're experts here,
As giggles ring, the day is clear.

With painted skin, we chase the light,
In this bright world, everything feels right.
A canvas filled with joy and glee,
Where sticky sweetness sets us free.

## Aromatic Adventures

With scents so sweet, they fill the air,
Each laugh and giggle, a fragrant flare.
We wander through this tasty maze,
Enchanted by these wondrous ways.

A basket full, with treasures rare,
Their colors bright, beyond compare.
From juicy bites to zesty sips,
In every mouthful, friendship dips.

As flavors burst, we cheer and sing,
A chorus of joy, our hearts take wing.
We dive right in, no fear in sight,
These savory dreams, oh what a delight!

Amidst the laughter, the sun shines bright,
Our bellies full, what a joyful sight.
With every nibble, we share a smile,
In this sweet moment, let's hang awhile.

## **A Festival of Flavors**

The table's set, a feast divine,
With vibrant hues that brightly shine.
We gather round, our hearts so light,
In every taste, pure sheer delight.

A splash of zest, a pop of fun,
As fruity games have just begun.
We chuckle loud, with juice-stained shirts,
In this wild world, where laughter flirts.

The neighbors peek, their faces wide,
As we enjoy this fruity ride.
We trade our slices, a barter made,
With every giggle, new memories laid.

The sun dips low, our voices rise,
As flavors dance beneath the skies.
We toast to fun, to joy, to play,
In this light-hearted, festive day.

## **Vibrant Echoes of Summer**

Echoes ring of joy and glee,
As summer whispers, wild and free.
With laughter spilling, bright and bold,
these memories weave, a tale retold.

In every bite, a story spun,
Of sunny skies and endless fun.
We gather here, in circles wide,
With every joy, our hearts reside.

The playful shouts, the splash of cheer,
An echo of love, so very near.
As laughter dances on the breeze,
We grab the day, we seize, we seize!

Our hands are sticky, our spirits high,
In this vibrant world, we laugh and fly.
With each bright taste, our souls ignite,
In this playful paradise, all feels right.

## **Wanderlust in Every Slice**

In a world of green and gold,
Slices call, both brave and bold.
Juicy laughter fills the air,
Travel tales, we love to share.

With every bite, a trip begins,
Chasing flavors, chasing sins.
A wanderer in every taste,
Adventure's never gone to waste.

Seeds like dreams, they scatter wide,
Life's a picnic, come join the ride.
Smiles burst with each surprise,
Wanderlust in sweet reprise.

Sticky fingers, happy grins,
In this feast, no one but wins.
Slice by slice, we roam afar,
Underneath the sunny star.

## **A Garden of Delight**

In a garden, bright and lush,
Fruity colors start to hush.
Squishy giggles, juicy spills,
Nature's laughter, pure and thrills.

Round the vines, the critters peek,
Chasing flavors, oh so sleek.
Running wild, like kids at play,
In this patch, we shout hooray!

Bouncing dreams from one to two,
Every slice is something new.
Picky eaters find their fate,
In this patch, there's no debate.

Sunshine melts the mundane days,
In this garden, hearts ablaze.
Sips of joy, from cups that gleam,
Nectar sweetness, life's sweet dream.

# The Poetry of Taste

Every nibble tells a tale,
Of summer days, and breeze's sail.
Beneath the sun's affectionate gaze,
We write our joy in sugary ways.

Chopping chunks with wild delight,
Bringing smiles, oh what a sight!
In this feast, the world's our stage,
Each bite, a poem, turn the page.

With every crunch, a giggle blooms,
Swirling laughs in tasty rooms.
Flavor verses, fresh and bright,
In this symphony of light.

So raise a slice, let laughter flow,
Together, let our spirits glow.
Tasting life, a jolly song,
With flavors, we all belong.

## Sweet Secrets in the Sun

Underneath the bright day shine,
Whispers of sweetness intertwine.
Laughter dances through the juice,
In this day, there's no excuse.

Sipping smiles, we bask and play,
In the warmth, the sun's ballet.
Secrets hidden in each slice,
Nature's gifts, oh so precise.

Happy munching, cheeks so round,
In this treasure, joy is found.
Beneath the shade, we chat and joke,
In this moment, laughter's woke.

So gather round, the friends we love,
Shower us with sunlight's shove.
Sweet secrets shared in silly fun,
On these days, we all are one.

## Green Horizons

In fields so vast, a sight so bright,
The green delight, a pure delight.
A juicy giggle, a playful jest,
Nature's laughter, a fruit-filled fest.

With seeds that dance and juicy cheer,
Oh, how we laugh when they appear!
Slips and slides, we tumble down,
In this sweet patch, we wear a crown.

A bite reveals a funny face,
As juice escapes, we quicken the pace.
A sticky hug from nature's bane,
In this merry land, joy's not in vain.

So here we play, with smiles all around,
In green horizons, our laughter's found.
A comical scene, so full of mirth,
In the heart of the land, where fun gives birth.

## Slice of Sunshine

A slice of cheer on a sunny morn,
With laughter fresh, the day is born.
Each juicy bite, a burst of glee,
As sunshine falls, we dance with tea.

Colorful plates of giggles and grins,
A fruity feast, let the fun begins.
We trade our woes for laughter's spree,
In slices bright, we feel so free.

The table's set with jokes galore,
As we munch away, we crave for more.
With every laugh, our worries fade,
In this slice of joy, pure fun is made.

So grab a plate and join the song,
In the sunlit bubbles, we all belong.
With laughter ripe, let the moments shine,
In a slice of happiness, all is fine.

## Watered Sunshine

Under the sun, we splash and play,
With watered joy, we chase the day.
Little giggles, a party loud,
In puddles created, we feel so proud.

The drips and drops are songs of glee,
In this merry dance, we run wild and free.
With brightened skies, our spirits soar,
Watered sunshine, who could ask for more?

Each spray of laughter, a silly plot,
As we toss our worries, it matters not.
From puddles deep, we jump and shout,
In this playful world, we twist about.

So let the moments flow like streams,
In sprinkled laughter, we share our dreams.
Watered sunshine, a joyous embrace,
In nature's fun, we find our place.

## Golden Petals

In gardens lush, with petals so bright,
Golden hues dance in the light.
A sprinkle of joy, a flower's grin,
In this patch of warmth, the fun begins.

We gather blooms, a playful quest,
With winks and giggles, we feel so blessed.
The colors shimmer, a canvas wide,
In this grassy realm, laughter can't hide.

Petals drop like confetti, oh what a sight!
As we twirl through petals, pure delight.
With every breeze, our chuckles soar,
In a garden of fun, who could ask for more?

So let's dance among these golden treats,
In the laughter-filled sway of nature's feats.
With petals in hand, we craft a tale,
In a garden of whimsy, we will prevail.

## Lush Fruits

In orchards ripe, where laughter grows,
Every step a tickle, as nature knows.
With juicy bites that burst with joy,
In the land of lush fruits, we feel the buoy.

We climb the trees, a silly race,
For the sun-kissed gems in this happy space.
With every pluck, a giggly cheer,
In this fruit-filled realm, we have no fear.

May the juice flow, with splashes and grins,
As we toss aside all our chagrins.
The laughter ripens, sweet and fun,
In the orchard of mirth, we all become one.

So join the feast, let the fun unfold,
In this lush paradise, our tales retold.
With sweet whispers of laughter and cheer,
In the orchard of joy, we find our sphere.

## Sunlit Secrets

In the patch where the laughter blooms,
Round and sweet, no sense of gloom.
Sunshine tickles the vibrant skin,
Joyous seeds are waiting within.

A squirrel sneaks with a cheeky grin,
Thinking he'll take one for a win.
But those fruits, they have a plan,
Rolling away as fast as they can!

Children giggle, their faces aglow,
As they run where the wild vines grow.
Their sticky hands, a sweetened mess,
Chasing dreams in a fruity dress.

Each bite bursts with a burst of cheer,
Whispers of secrets for all to hear.
Smiles and sweetness, not a trace of woe,
In the sunshine's warm, golden glow.

## The Dance of Juicy Delights

Round and plump, they bounce and sway,
In the sun, they laugh and play.
Rolling like stars, a fruity parade,
Every borborygmus is serenade.

With a wink, the cucumbers prance,
While stands of corn join in the dance.
Tomatoes blush in a salsa swirl,
As peaches giggle in a soft twirl.

The farmers chuckle, hands on their hips,
Watching all the juicy flips.
What a sight, this veggie show,
A harvest of giggles, don't you know?

Under the moon, the folly won't cease,
With crunchy munching, they share their peace.
Delights abound in the garden's embrace,
A fun-filled night in this jolly place!

## Garden's Bounty

Laughter ripens in every row,
Where vines weave tales with a playful flow.
Gather 'round for the banquet tied,
To stories spun in the garden wide.

Carts collide with giggles loud,
As berries blush and the squash is proud.
Pumpkins tumble, laughing quite bright,
In this green realm, all feels just right.

Sneaky sprouts bring a comic twist,
'Cause something funny always exists.
With every harvest, we celebrate,
In this produce party, it's never too late.

Blooms like confetti, tossed in the breeze,
As we munch our treasures with silly ease.
In the garden's warmth, hearts grow buoyant,
In juicy revelry, we stay radiant!

## A Splash of Summer


Under the sun, the fun begins,
With juicy drizzles and fruity spins.
Waves of laughter in a splashy race,
As watermelons roll with daring grace.

Outrageous flavors leap and dive,
In a contest as juicy as they strive.
Each twist and turn a giggle's delight,
Chasing summer under starlit night.

With every slice, a splash of cheer,
Sweet juice flowing, no hint of fear.
Clumsy hands catch the colorful spree,
In this fruity circus, just wait and see!

So raise your cups for the summer fun,
As laughter dances and the day is won.
Every drop brings a smile so bright,
In this joyous, juicy summer light!

## Summer's Embrace

Beneath the sun's bright, shining rays,
We dance around in laughter's haze.
A sticky treat drips down our chin,
We yell for joy with every spin.

The colors burst like fireworks bright,
Each juicy slice is pure delight.
With every bite, we squeal with glee,
Who knew a fruit could make us free?

We wear our smiles like crowns so bold,
Sharing stories wild and old.
Oh, these sweet moments in the heat,
They're like a snack that's hard to beat!

As the sun sets in the sky,
We sip on joy, and time goes by.
With belly laughs and spritzing juice,
Our fondest days, we can't excuse.

## The Orchard's Song

In orchards lush, we find our play,
Chasing shadows, come what may.
The fruits hang low, a tempting sight,
We reach for joy with all our might.

Each crunchy bite and giggles shared,
In every laugh, our hearts are bared.
Oh, how we dance beneath the trees,
With juicy spoils and swings of ease!

The bees hum tunes, we sing along,
Life tastes better when it's a song.
Our worries fade; we're carefree clowns,
In this green realm, we lose our frowns.

With every step, the earth feels warm,
In laughter's grip, we find our charm.
The sun-kissed days, we'll hold them dear,
In pockets full of summer cheer.

## Delights of the Warmth

When heat arrives, we rush outside,
On warm, green grass, we take a ride.
The flavors burst, a wild surprise,
We revel in the sunny skies.

With every scoop, we laugh and play,
The world feels bright, come what may.
Oh, sticky hands and gooey grins,
Each silly dance, the joy begins!

A picnic feast, absurdly grand,
We juggle fruits with careless hands.
The dog runs past, with funny barks,
Our laughter echoes through the parks.

As twilight comes, our spirits high,
We toast to days that never die.
In every drop of sweat we find,
The essence of a summer's mind.

## **Vibrant Nectar**

In gardens bright with colors bold,
We pluck the treats, a tale untold.
The juice runs wild, we squeal and shout,
Adventure lurks in every pout.

Our sticky fingers, sweet and glazed,
Each silly stumble leaves us dazed.
Giggles burst like bubbles high,
In this warm swirl, we feel we fly.

Ah, the flavors dance upon the tongue,
The trickster trees have us all strung.
We laugh at how we've lost our way,
In nature's charm, we choose to stay.

As daylight fades, the stars turn bright,
In vivid dreams, we'll take our flight.
For every moment that we revel,
Life's a joke, and we're the level.

## A Symphony of Summer Flavors

In the sunlit garden, laughter blooms,
Juicy drips from cheerful spoons.
Belly laughs with every bite,
Sticky fingers feel so right.

Taste buds dance, a sweet parade,
In the shade, their fears allayed.
Chasing joy, we munch and play,
Wishing for this snack-filled day.

Colors burst like fireworks bright,
On the picnic cloth, delight takes flight.
Slurping, giggles fill the air,
Messy faces, without a care.

With each slice, a tale unspooled,
Childhood dreams, delightfully fueled.
Making memories with every cheer,
The sweetest times of the whole year.

## **The Art of Refreshment**

A splash of fun in every bite,
Chilled concoctions, pure delight.
Sipping smiles from cups so wide,
Who knew fruits could be this spry?

The blender hums a merry tune,
In the kitchen, chaos is strewn.
Whirling colors spin with flair,
Happiness fills the humid air.

Shaking jars with patient hearts,
Artistry in fruit-filled parts.
Mixing highs with crazy lows,
Creating masterpieces where sweetness flows.

With every twist and twirl, we find,
Pure refreshment—truly divine!
Laughter freezes, time stands still,
In our cups, we sip our thrill.

## Bright Horizons on the Table

A vibrant spread, joy's delight,
Colors dance under sunlight.
Beside the daisies, laughter rings,
With every bite, a joy it brings.

Forks and spoons, a playful clink,
Between the bites, we pause to think.
What shall we taste? What's next in line?
Cherries burst with a taste so fine.

Stories shared with sticky hands,
Outside, the world with warmth expands.
An artful mess, a sight to see,
As life unfolds so joyfully.

Under trees, we bask and feast,
Savoring each silly beast.
Bright horizons, life so grand,
On this table, all is planned.

## **Flavorful Reminisces of Youth**

A colorful plate, a tale in taste,
Summers breezed, never chaste.
Running wild, our hearts ablaze,
Snack attacks on sunny days.

Whispers shared through crumbs and giggles,
As time with friends always wiggles.
Tasting dreams from fields so wide,
Flavorful trips—a joyride.

Sun-kissed cheeks and vibrant hues,
Nostalgic moments, nothing to lose.
Each bite a memory, pure and sweet,
In our hearts, life's luscious treat.

Those playful days, forever blend,
With every bite, we don't pretend.
Laughter rings through orchard trees,
Flavorful echoes on the breeze.

## Radiant and Round

In the garden, they giggle, so round,
Bouncing on vines, they tumble and bound.
A splash of green, a sunlit charm,
They tease the dogs, causing alarm.

Pies and juices, a summer delight,
Rolling off tables in joyful flight.
Children squeal with sticky hands,
As laughter echoes across the lands.

A slice shared, with tales spun wide,
Orange sun setting, it's time to slide.
With every bite, the world feels right,
Whispers of sweetness dance in the night.

In the basket, a treasure of fun,
Shiny and plump, basking in sun.
A fruit-filled tale that never ends,
Colors of joy that nature sends.

## Lush Lullabies at Dusk

Under the stars, they sing and sway,
Crickets join in, creating the play.
Whispers of green with giggles abound,
A luscious treat that spins round and round.

The evening breeze carries scents so sweet,
Footprints trailing, shuffling feet.
Nature hums a tune of cheer,
Lively laughter flowing near.

Chasing shadows, what a sight,
In the twilight, they take flight.
Round they roll, high spirits bloom,
Beneath the watchful moon's silver loom.

As dusk wraps the day in hues,
Everyone shares their favorite views.
With memories stitched in each bright sound,
In the laughter of night, joy is found.

# The Flavor of Warmth

In the kitchen, aromas swirl and dance,
Friends gather 'round for a taste of chance.
A pot of goodness, bubbling away,
Promises of laughter at the end of the day.

Sticky fingers reaching for more,
A rainbow of flavors to happily explore.
Each spoonful brings forth a delighted cheer,
Warmth shared amongst everyone here.

Who knew, in sunshine's warm embrace,
The kitchen could be such a magical place?
With silly jokes and stories that play,
Moments of bliss, we cherish and stay.

When the feast finally graces the table,
Silly hats worn, we're quite the fable.
Food and friends in a raucous parade,
A sweet tapestry of joy we've made.

## Nature's Sweet Canvas

In the orchard where giggles bloom,
Colors splash in a playful room.
Round and vibrant, they catch the eye,
Nature's palette beneath the sky.

Patterns of chaos, a feast for all,
Bouncing and rolling, they have a ball.
Sticky smiles and laughter that plays,
Memories woven through sunlit rays.

The canvas drips with hues so bright,
As they paint the ground with pure delight.
Picnics scattered on blankets laid,
Savoring flavors that never fade.

Under the trees, tales begin,
With every bite, a new grin.
Art of joy in a wobbly dance,
Nature's laughter, a merry chance.

www.ingramcontent.com/pod-product-compliance
Lightning Source LLC
Chambersburg PA
CBHW050305120526
44590CB00016B/2498